Pets

Tina Hearne

Illustrated by
Craig Austin

Kingfisher Books

Contents

Edited by Alan Wakeford
Illustrated by Craig Austin/The Garden Studio

This edition published in 1986 by
Kingfisher Books Ltd, Elsley Court,
20–22 Great Titchfield Street,
London W1P 7AD
A Grisewood & Dempsey Company
First published in 1986 in paperback in the
Piccolo Spotters series by Piper Books Ltd.
© Grisewood & Dempsey Ltd 1986
All rights reserved

Phototypeset by Waveney Typesetters, Norwich
Printed and bound in Portugal by Printer Portuguesa

BRITISH LIBRARY CATALOGUING IN PUBLICATION DATA
Hearne, Tina
   Pets.—(Kingfisher fun-to-spot series)
   1. Pets—Juvenile literature
   I. Title   II. Austin, Craig
   636.08'87   SF416.2

ISBN 0 86272 235 7

Introduction

This book will help you to identify the animals most often kept as family pets, as well as some of the breeds or varieties of each species. It will encourage you to observe the habits of the animals and their physical condition. Finally, it will tell you how they should be fed, watered, handled, sheltered and exercised.

Always be quiet and gentle when you approach animals. Use your eyes to make the most of your observations, and do not touch other people's pets unless invited. Animals have feelings too and may be alarmed by strangers. If they are frightened they may strike out and bite or scratch.

It is important not to rush into pet-keeping yourself unless you have understood the difficulties as well as the pleasures of having animals. Good spotters are trained observers and are therefore likely to be good pet-keepers. For instance, once you get used to the way in which your pet looks and behaves in good health, you will quickly recognize the first signs of ill-health, and know when to consult a veterinary surgeon.

Those of you who do choose to keep a pet of your own will discover that the book holds information on the biology and natural history of each kind of animal. This is useful, because once you know how these animals live in the wild, you will have a better idea of their needs when they are kept as pets.

Whenever possible, captive animals should be allowed to do what comes naturally to them. Of course, everything has to be on a smaller scale. However, birds should still be able to fly, and fish need to be able to swim in a reasonable space. Hamsters and gerbils should have what they need to dig and burrow, even when kept as pets. Good pet-keepers will understand these needs and save their animals the long hours of boredom from which so many pets suffer.

Dogs and Cats

Dogs run fast, but they are not able to climb trees as cats can. Dogs are active in the day-time, but most cats, given the chance, choose to roam around at night. Dogs like to be together in a pack, and some hunt that way, but cats are solitary animals and hunt alone. Dogs bark, but cats mew.

You may often have noticed differences between dogs and cats, but in this book they are grouped together because they are similar in one very important way. Dogs and cats are carnivores. The word means 'flesh-eaters'. Long before they were domesticated and kept by people, the wild ancestors of our pet dogs and cats found their own food. They hunted for small rodents and other mammals, amphibians, birds and fish. The dogs took low-growing fruits and berries too.

The teeth of all the carnivores are specially adapted for killing and eating their prey. The most noticeable teeth are the fangs—the canines—which are used as a weapon and for tearing flesh. These teeth are so big in dogs that they take their name from the Latin word for a dog, *canis*, but cats also have powerful canine teeth.

In captivity, cats can live on an entirely carnivorous diet of meat, fish and offal. Dogs do best if they are given some cereal food with their meat—dog biscuit, dog meal or wholemeal bread baked into hard rusks. It is not necessary to feed healthy, adult dogs and cats on meat that has been minced or cut small. The animals are quite capable of tearing food for themselves. The exercise is good for their teeth and gums. For the same reason, hard biscuits or chews, or a big, safe marrow bone can be given to a dog.

Dogs and cats will always try to meet up with other dogs and cats for mating. If they are successful, a bitch will have two litters a year, and a cat may have two or three litters, although there are probably not enough

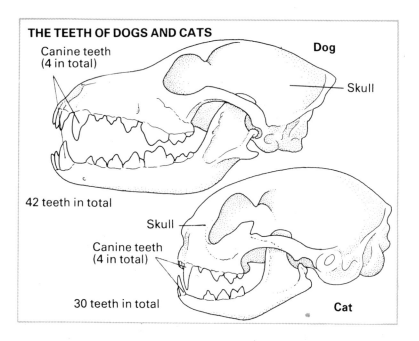

THE TEETH OF DOGS AND CATS

Dog

Canine teeth
(4 in total)

Skull

42 teeth in total

Skull

Canine teeth
(4 in total)

30 teeth in total

Cat

good homes for all the puppies and kittens. The best way to prevent unwanted pregnancies is to arrange for a veterinary surgeon to neuter female dogs and cats while they are young. After they have been spayed, animals cannot become pregnant.

Most owners have male cats neutered. After neutering there is a change in their behaviour that makes them less liable to roam, and to spray urine in the house in order to mark their territory. Some male dogs are neutered, too, making them less likely to wander, less aggressive, and easier to train.

Serious diseases can be passed from dog to dog, and from cat to cat. Because dogs and cats mix with others of their kind, they run the risk of catching and dying from one of these infections. All puppies and kittens can be protected if they are given a course of vaccinations starting, usually, at the age of 10 to 12 weeks. When they are older, they will need the extra protection of booster injections.

DOGS

Dogs have been kept by people for about 10,000 years. Since then, many breeds have been developed. In the past, each breed was kept for a particular purpose; now most are kept as pets.

There are three categories of sporting breeds: hounds, terriers and gundogs. And there are also three categories of non-sporting breeds: utility dogs, working dogs and toy breeds.

There are about 200 breeds for you to begin spotting, as well as crossbreds and mongrels. Crossbreds are the result of a dam (female) and sire (male) of different breeds mating together and producing puppies displaying some of the characteristics of each parent. Mongrels are the dogs of mixed ancestry. They show muddled characteristics of several breeds, but are usually very strong and even tempered. These animals can make ideal pets.

AFGHAN HOUND

This is a very old breed, known in Ancient Egypt, which was brought to Europe from Afghanistan. It was well-suited to hunting in hill country, using its excellent vision. Like the Saluki and Greyhound it is now classed as a *sight hound*. It is swift and powerful, with the right build to jump obstacles.

Another group, the *scent hounds*, such as the Bassett and Beagle, are short-legged, and usually hunt in a pack following a scent trail on the ground.

GOLDEN RETRIEVER

The Golden Retriever is a good-natured, beautiful dog, and very popular as a pet. Originally it was bred as a gun dog and is particularly known for its skill in retrieving from water. Any dog capable of sustained hard work must be given lots of exercise when kept as a pet. *All* dogs must be kept on a lead near traffic, and in the country near sheep or other livestock they may be tempted to chase.

AIREDALE TERRIER

The terriers are hunting dogs trained to chase their quarry from its hole. The Airedale is the largest terrier, and known as the best rat catcher of all. It is a smart and alert dog with a wiry coat of black and tan (illustrated) or grey and tan. It needs lots of exercise. For short periods in between, a running chain will keep the dog secure while giving it some limited freedom.

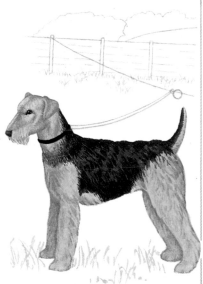

POODLE

A highly intelligent, companionable dog, the Poodle is bred in three sizes: Standard, Miniature, and Toy. It is classed as a utility dog, i.e. one bred for a special purpose, but not included in the working or sporting categories. The Dalmatian is another utility breed once used as a carriage escort.

The Poodle was bred as a performing dog, but has also been used to retrieve from water. Its quick-growing coat needs regular trimming and grooming.

PEKINGESE

This is another ancient breed, known in China 2000 years ago, and was brought to Europe in the 19th century. It was bred as a lap dog, needing little exercise, but the coat, which is long and straight, requires a great deal of grooming. Like many short-faced dogs, the Pekingese may be troubled by such ailments as tartar on overcrowded teeth, skin irritations in the folds of skin on the face and breathing disorders. The prominent eyes also make the breed liable to eye damage.

GERMAN SHEPHERD DOG

The German Shepherd Dog was previously known as the Alsatian. It belongs to the category of working dogs and was originally used as a herding dog in Germany. Now, however, it is more often kept as a guard-dog, and its sensitive nose and outstanding courage and stamina make it a good police dog.

The German Shepherd is a popular pet, but often is kept in too small an area. A big, intelligent, energetic animal, it needs plenty of space, exercise and training.

WELSH CORGIS

These are working dogs traditionally used for herding cattle. There are two breeds: Cardigan and Pembroke, distinguished by their tails. The Cardigan Corgi has a normal tail; the Pembroke Corgi has its tail docked (cut off or cut short). The strange habit of docking is still practised in Britain, although some veterinary surgeons now refuse to perform the operation.

CATS

Cats were domesticated about 4000 years ago in Ancient Egypt, where they were a highly respected animal. Although the Egyptians tried to keep their cats to themselves, eventually some were smuggled out of the country, and domestic cats became known in Europe from Roman times. During the Middle Ages they were not so popular in Europe. They became identified with witchcraft, and were thought unlucky. Their wonderful skill as mousers and ratters did not save them from cruel treatment. Happily, cats became more popular again in the 18th and 19th centuries, and are now one of our best loved pet animals.

Most cats are mongrel, but there are about 100 breeds for you to begin to recognize. To make it easier for you the breeds can be grouped into three basic types: British (or European) Short-haired, Foreign Short-haired, and Long-haired cats.

BRITISH SHORT-HAIRED – BI-COLOURED

The British Short-haired cats are strong and sturdy in build, with short legs. The head is rounded, with big, wide-set eyes, and small, wide-set ears. The cheeks are full and the nose small. Self-coloured (single-coloured) Short-hairs include the Black, White, Cream, and Blue. The cats with patches of two colours are known as bi-coloured. Black and White (illustrated) is common, but any colour may be seen with white.

BRITISH SHORT-HAIRED — MACKEREL TABBY

The Mackerel, or Striped Tabby is the oldest pattern found among domestic cats. Traces of it show on new-born kittens of other breeds, and even on self-coloured cats. The markings tend to fade as the kitten grows.

Mackerel markings should be in the form of dense, narrow stripes around the body, the legs and the tail.

BRITISH SHORT-HAIRED — STANDARD TABBY

This differently marked Tabby is the Standard or Blotched Tabby. Its most distinctive mark is the blotch or whorl on the flanks.

The Standard Tabby appeared in Europe several hundred years ago. It developed out of the older breed of Mackerel Tabby.

LONG-HAIRED – TORTOISESHELL AND WHITE

This is a four-colour cat. The colouring is black, red, cream and white. Like all the Long-haired breeds, the body is thick-set and short-legged. The head is wide, and the coat and tail long and thick.

All the Long-haired breeds need daily grooming, and show cats are groomed several times every day.

FOREIGN SHORT-HAIRED – SIAMESE

The outline of the Foreign Short-haired breeds is angular, lean and long-legged, with pointed face and tail. These are the Orientals – Burmese, Abyssinian, and Siamese.

New-born Siamese show no markings. The dark 'points' (ears, feet, legs and tail) and face mask begin to show only as the kittens grow.

The animals illustrated are the Cream Point (left), Seal Point (middle) and Chocolate Point (right).

LONG-HAIRED – CHINCHILLA

The Americans call this lovely cat the Silver. The colour is the result of pure white hairs on the back, flanks, head and tail being tipped with black, giving a silver effect. The fur of the chest and stomach is pure white. The ears are tufted with white. Chinchilla kittens are born much darker, with tabby markings that fade with age.

Rabbits and Rodents

Rabbits and rodents are gnawing animals, with teeth specially adapted for the purpose. The front teeth—the incisors—are big, strong and chisel shaped. They also grow continually, like finger nails, and so never wear away no matter how much the animal has to gnaw.

You will notice the heading of this section of the book is 'Rabbits and Rodents' and not simply 'Rodents'. There is a biological reason for this. The rabbits may seem very like the rodents, but in fact are classed with the hares as a different order of animals—the lagomorphs. Once, however, rabbits were called 'double-toothed rodents', and the diagram shows you why. Notice the double row of incisor teeth in the upper jaw. This feature is common to both rabbits and hares, but the rodents lack the second row of incisors.

The rabbits and rodents are mainly herbivorous (plant-eating), and while some can live exclusively on grasses, others will feed on the hardest vegetable matter, such as tough roots and nuts. In captivity, it is important to offer plenty of fresh drinking water, particularly when dry foods such as grains form a large part of their diet.

It is also important to provide good bedding materials for these animals, and a place where they can seek privacy. All of them tend to be timid, and like to conceal themselves at times. They should not have to live fully exposed. This is particularly true of the nocturnal rodents such as the hamsters which, in the wild, sleep underground during the day and rarely see daylight.

Since they can gnaw their way out of confinement, the rabbits and rodents have to be provided with accommodation that is very secure. It helps to line the hutches and cages with Formica or plywood so that the animals are presented with a smooth interior which is difficult to begin to gnaw. If the timber framework of a hutch or cage is exposed, it will soon be attacked.

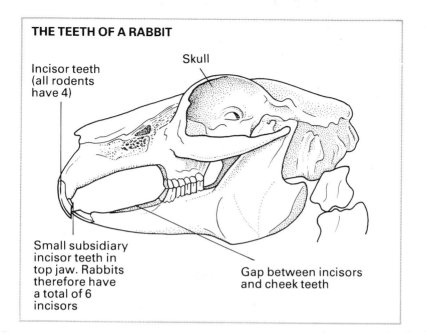

THE TEETH OF A RABBIT

Incisor teeth (all rodents have 4)

Skull

Small subsidiary incisor teeth in top jaw. Rabbits therefore have a total of 6 incisors

Gap between incisors and cheek teeth

Although these animals need to be discouraged from gnawing their own accommodation, they must be given logs and branches to gnaw to keep their teeth trim. In captivity, overgrown incisors can become a problem and will eventually prevent the animal from feeding properly. Do not worry about a pet swallowing splinters. Rabbits and rodents gnaw with the cheeks drawn into the gap between the incisors and the back teeth. This forms a barrier, and prevents splinters from being swallowed.

The most challenging task, for the owner of a rabbit or a rodent, is to give the pet plenty of exercise and an interesting place to live, while keeping it secure. A three-cornered grazing cage, with chicken wire on the base as well as the sides, is one solution for the rabbits and guinea-pigs. The ark can be moved around the garden to provide fresh grazing each day. If a roof is provided at one end, the animals will then have some adequate shelter from the rain and sun.

RABBITS

Rabbits originally came from Spain and Portugal. They have been known throughout most of Europe since Roman times, although records of the rabbit in Britain go back only to the 12th century. In modern times, the rabbit has been introduced to other continents, notably Australia, where it thrived so much, having no natural enemies, that it became a pest.

Originally, the rabbit was kept in Britain for its meat and for its fur. Only recently has it been bred as a pet and an animal for the show-bench.

There are about 35 breeds of rabbit, and they can be grouped into three main types.

The normal fur breeds have the same sort of coat as the wild rabbit. The fancy breeds are novelties that have been bred primarily for showing. The Rex and Satin breeds have short, dense coats because the long guard hairs are absent.

ORANGE REX

The normal coat of a wild rabbit has short underhairs and longer, coarser 'guard hairs'. In the Rex breeds, the longer guard hairs are absent. The coat is soft and short, rather like velvet. The Rex breeds have been skilfully bred from a rabbit born with the different length of coat. Such an animal, varying from the normal, is called a mutant if it can pass on its special characteristic to future generations.

NORMAL FUR BREED – NEW ZEALAND WHITE

This very large rabbit, weighing around 5.5 kg, like the Californian, was originally bred for its meat. Sheer size makes the New Zealand difficult for children to handle, and so it may not be the best choice for a pet.

It is very cruel to keep any rabbit shut up all the time, and particularly the larger breeds. They need plenty of freedom to exercise in safety.

NORMAL FUR BREED – CHINCHILLA

This is one of the rabbits originally bred for its fur. Others include the Silver Fox and the Sables. These rabbits have fur which imitates the coat of the animal they are named after. In this case it is the Chinchilla, which is a small South American rodent, with intermingled black and white hairs, giving a silver effect.

FANCY BREED – ANGORA

Most rabbits are able to groom themselves adequately. The exception is the Angora, which needs daily brushing.

This is a medium-sized rabbit, bred not for its fur, but for its wool. The Angora coat is made up of long guard hairs intermingled in a dense undercoat of wool. When the rabbit is kept especially for its wool, it is clipped every few months, and the coat then left to grow again.

Its beautiful coat also makes the Angora a popular rabbit for showing.

FANCY BREED – DUTCH RABBIT

The Dutch rabbit is one of the fancy breeds with distinctive body markings. It is the result of careful breeding from mutants. The Black and White is pictured here, and was the first colour combination bred, but now any colour may be seen with white.

This is a small rabbit of about 2.2 kg, and makes an excellent pet. It is easy to handle and has a gentle nature.

FANCY BREED – ENGLISH RABBIT

The English rabbit is a very popular breed dating from the 19th century. It is quite a big rabbit of about 4 kg. The

Black and White is common, but the markings include other colours on white.

Breeders pay much attention to the pattern of the markings. Look for a dark ridge along the spine, dark ears, dark circles around the eyes, dark spots on the face, and dark markings on the flanks. There should also be a butterfly-shaped mark on the nose.

FANCY BREED – NETHERLAND DWARF

These animals are the smallest of the rabbit breeds, weighing as little as 1 kg. They are very suitable and popular as pets, since they are easy to handle and have a gentle nature.

Look out not only for the self colours, but also for those with patterned coats such as the Dutch.

19

GUINEA PIGS

The guinea pig, or cavy, is a South American animal that was brought to Europe by sailors in the 16th century. In South America it lives in grassland, and although it may seek shelter in rocks and caves, it does not burrow. Its diet is almost entirely grass, and it hides from predatory birds by moving around in surface tunnels trodden through the grass.

In captivity, the guinea pig must be fed mainly on grass or hay (i.e. dried grass), with some leaf and root vegetables for variety. Grain replaces the seeding grasses they would eat in the wild.

As rodents, they must be given the chance to gnaw and so wear down their growing teeth. The claws, too, need to be worn down by exercising sometimes on a hard surface.

The different breeds of guinea pig are grouped, according to coat-type, into three distinct varieties: the Smooth-haired, the Rough-haired and the Long-haired.

SMOOTH-HAIRED – DUTCH GUINEA PIG

The Smooth- or Short-haired guinea pig is also known as the English or the Bolivian cavy. There are various self colours, including black, white, blue, red, cream, beige, golden, chocolate and lilac. This breed also occurs in a variety of patterns. One is the Himalayan, with dark points rather like a Siamese cat. Another is the Dutch, seen here, marked like a Dutch rabbit. Any colour may be seen with white.

ROUGH-HAIRED – ABYSSINIAN

The wild guinea pigs are short haired, but in captivity certain mutations have developed and have been kept by careful breeding. The Abyssinian is the result of a mutation. The hair stands up and is arranged in rosettes or whorls all over the body. A prize Abyssinian will have ten rosettes in all. When only two or three are seen, the guinea pig or its ancestors will have been crossbred from an Abyssinian/ Smooth-haired mating.

LONG-HAIRED – PERUVIAN

The Long-haired guinea pig is known as the Peruvian. Again, it is bred from a mutant. Peruvians may be found in the whole range of colours, including the Tortoiseshell and White, as illustrated. The hair falls from a centre parting along the spine, and may grow to 1 metre in length.

The young are most appealing. After a long pregnancy of about 63 days, they are born with fur and with their eyes open.

HAMSTERS

The Golden hamster, which is now a very popular pet, is native to the deserts of Syria. It survives in the wild only by avoiding the heat of the sun. During the day, the wild hamsters rest underground in their burrows, emerging only at night to collect scattered, wind-blown seeds that are their food. It is at night, when they travel many kilometres in search of food, that they need the protection of their fur, for the desert nights can be very cold.

Pet hamsters are thought to have derived from a single female and her litter found in Syria in 1930 when zoologists thought the species extinct. About 30 colour varieties now exist.

Hamsters are solitary animals, and therefore one of the few pet animals that must be kept singly. They will fight to the death if caged together. Unless you are an expert it is never advisable to breed hamsters because they are extremely difficult to pair up, even for mating.

GOLDEN HAMSTER

This is the hamster nearest in colour to the wild species. The hamster is a rich golden brown over the head, back and flanks, with a white underside. There is a dark cheek flash either side of the face.

These animals become very tame when handled often. In between times, they must be given as interesting a home as possible, where they can burrow, gnaw and rest in privacy.

CINNAMON BANDED

Any self colour may be banded in this way. The band of white fur separates the self colour into two parts.

Hamsters tend to 'pouch' their food and carry it in the cheeks to the hidden food store. It is normal for a hamster to hoard food, and the store should not be disturbed unless necessary. The hamster will eat at night, when it is active, more readily than during the day.

BLACK-EYED CREAM

This lovely hamster is feeding on its favourite food, the sunflower seed.

In captivity, it is a good idea to provide a solid exercise wheel, like the one illustrated, so that the animal gets plenty of exercise. It also needs wood to gnaw on, as well as hard foods like seeds, in order to keep its teeth trim.

GERBILS

The Mongolian gerbil has been kept as a pet in Europe since the 1960s. Before that time it was used as a laboratory animal in Japan and America.

This species of gerbil is native to the desert country of Mongolia, and to the northern provinces of China. It was first seen by Europeans in the 19th century when a French naturalist recorded it as a 'yellow rat', with black claws and a black tuft at the tip of its tail.

Like the hamster, the Mongolian gerbil only survives in the desert by burrowing underground to escape the heat of the sun. During the winter, when the desert is hidden beneath snow, the gerbil may have to live entirely underground for several months feeding only on hoarded food.

There has not yet been time for many mutations to occur in captivity, but several colour varieties have appeared.

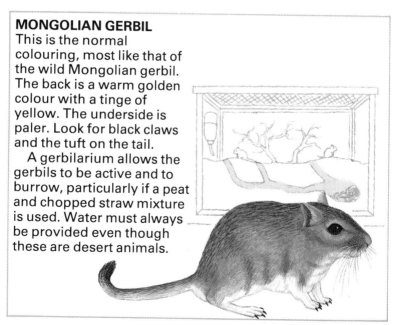

MONGOLIAN GERBIL
This is the normal colouring, most like that of the wild Mongolian gerbil. The back is a warm golden colour with a tinge of yellow. The underside is paler. Look for black claws and the tuft on the tail.

A gerbilarium allows the gerbils to be active and to burrow, particularly if a peat and chopped straw mixture is used. Water must always be provided even though these are desert animals.

MONGOLIAN GERBIL – ALBINO

Breeders always find that the Albino is one of the first mutations to occur in any breeding programme. The colour pigment is entirely missing, resulting in pink eyes, pale claws and white fur. Although popular in its own right, the Albino has been most useful to breeders in creating new colour varieties by cross breeding.

MONGOLIAN GERBIL – BLACK

This gerbil is really the opposite of the Albino, with an excess of black colouring pigment. It is another mutation which breeders were anxious to find because it allowed them to extend the colour range still further. The Black first occurred in America, but strict British quarantine laws delayed its arrival in this country.

MICE AND RATS

Fancy rats have been bred from the Common or Brown rat, while fancy mice have been bred from the house mouse. Both were first bred as laboratory animals, but have now become popular pets, despite their unpopular wild ancestors.

Mice and rats adapt well to cage-living, but it is important to allow them to get out of sight in their own cage. A nest box with nesting material is a good idea.

Never mix mice and rats in the same cage. Two male rats will usually live peaceably together—rats may also be kept singly, but would then need plenty of human company and exercise out of the cage. Female mice may be kept together in a small colony. Male mice will fight together, and should be housed singly from the age of five weeks. Avoid housing the sexes together, because both rats and mice breed freely with a short pregnancy of only 20–22 days.

BROKEN-MARKED MICE

About 40 breeds of mouse are now recognized, including many self colours and marked varieties. There are also long-haired and curly-coated mice. The Broken-marked mice seen here are quite common. They are expert climbers, so provide ropes and ladders for exercise.

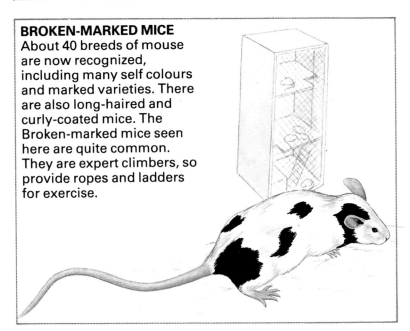

DUTCH MICE

The Dutch mice, marked exactly as a Dutch rabbit, may be Black and White, or any of the colours with white.

A solid exercise wheel gives these very active creatures some opportunity for exercise. Avoid a wheel with open spokes in which the tail or feet can become caught. Handle mice frequently and gently to make them tame enough to exercise out of the cage.

FAWN HOODED RAT

Self-coloured rats may be white, black, chocolate, fawn, or cream. The Hooded rat is a bi-coloured animal with a hood of one of the self colours extending down the line of the spine. Illustrated is the Fawn Hooded rat.

Rats, mice, and all the rodents need wood to gnaw in order to keep their teeth trim. The rats also like a length of piping in the cage, which they use as a ready-made burrow.

Birds

The two species of foreign birds which have become most successful as pets are the budgerigar and the canary. The budgerigar is a parrot, and will use its beak in climbing, as well as its toes. The canary is a finch, and a perching bird. Both species are seed-eaters and remove the outer husk from the seed before eating.

Although cages are often used for accommodation, both are social flock-birds, and are best kept in an aviary. Here they can have some free flight and be with others of their kind. This is particularly true for the canary, which may be too nervous to leave its cage for exercise. If budgerigars are caged, they must be given freedom to leave the cage for exercise at least once a day.

Never keep budgerigars and canaries together in the same accommodation. The more robust budgerigars may bully the delicate canary. Suitable aviary companions for the canary include the Java sparrow, the weavers and zebra finches. The budgerigar can safely share an aviary with small species of parakeet.

Feeding

Feeding is made simple because good pre-packed seed mixtures are readily available. Those prepared specially for canaries contain a higher proportion of rich seeds such as linseed and rape. In addition, offer both birds bunches of seeding grasses and some fresh greenstuff such as lettuce.

Water must be available at all times, although budgerigars may not drink as frequently as canaries. And both species can be given grit, cuttlefish 'bone' and a mineral block.

Breeding

For breeding, each pair of budgerigars must be provided with a nest box, for they are not nest-builders. Canaries

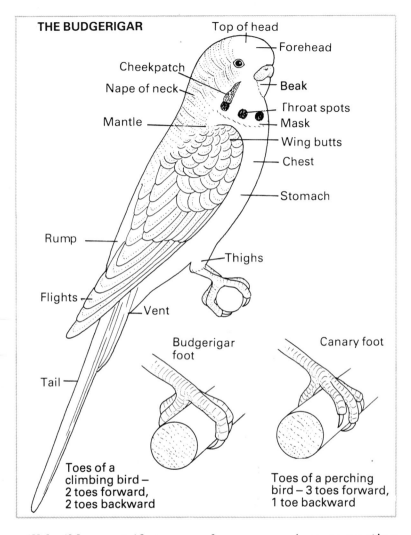

THE BUDGERIGAR

Top of head

Forehead

Cheekpatch

Nape of neck

Beak

Mantle

Throat spots

Mask

Wing butts

Chest

Stomach

Rump

Thighs

Flights

Vent

Budgerigar foot

Canary foot

Tail

Toes of a climbing bird – 2 toes forward, 2 toes backward

Toes of a perching bird – 3 toes forward, 1 toe backward

will build a nest if straw and moss are given as nesting materials, together with a nest pan.

Red birds are much sought after. Breeders do not expect a red budgerigar to occur, but canary breeders have introduced the red colour through 'hybridization'— that is, by crossing the canary with another species, the Red Hooded Siskin.

BUDGERIGARS

The budgerigar is native to Australia. It is a flock-bird of the dry, semi-desert country of the interior. Wild budgerigars feed on seeding grasses and drink, whenever they can, from water-holes that fill up from natural reservoirs of underground water. Sometimes there are heavy thunderstorms, and then the budgerigars feed on lush green shoots that spring up after the rain. Budgerigars fly a great deal in search of water, fresh pastures and breeding grounds. Every year they migrate (travel in search of more suitable temperatures) from the tropical heat of the north of the continent to the cooler area of the Murray–Darling rivers. Here they lay their eggs in holes in the gnarled, stunted eucalyptus trees. Often the birds enlarge a hole by pecking at it.

In the 19th century, Victorian travellers discovered the budgerigars. They netted the birds on the ground and brought them back to sell in Europe.

BUDGERIGAR COLOURS

There are three shades of each colour depending on the 'dark factor'. A bird with no dark factor will be a light colour. A bird which inherits one dark factor will be a medium colour. A bird which inherits dark factors from both parents will have the strongest colour.

Right: Ideally keep budgerigars in an outside aviary where there is space for them to exercise properly. There should also be shelter to protect them from the weather.

Blue Series	White Series	Green Series	Yellow Series
No dark factor			
Sky Blue	White Sky Blue	Light Green	Light Yellow
One dark factor			
Cobalt	White Cobalt	Dark Green	Dark Yellow
Two dark factors			
Mauve	White Mauve	Olive Green	Olive Yellow

LIGHT GREEN

The Light Green is the natural colour of the wild budgerigar. The head, mask (face), shoulders and wings are yellow. The six throat spots, the head and wing markings are black.

Sometimes, in Australia, a Yellow, for instance, will be seen flying with a flock of Light Greens. In captivity, such mutants are carefully preserved by skilled breeding. In the wild, the flock always tends to revert to the natural Light Green.

ALBINO AND LUTINO

The Albino is a budgerigar of the blue or white series, born without any colouring pigment. The lack of pigment removes all blue and black colour, leaving only the white ground.

The green and yellow series have a yellow ground colour. This remains when all the green and black is lacking. This form of budgerigar is a Lutino.

Both birds have red eyes due to a lack of pigment.

CINNAMON GREY

The range of basic colours is increased by the Grey, Slate, and Violet factors. These, too, occur in three shades because of the dark factor.

More variety still is gained because certain mutations reduce the black markings of the head and wings. Clearwings have no such markings; Cinnamons have the markings reduced to an attractive soft brown, as illustrated here.

PIED BUDGERIGARS

The breeding of Pied birds extends the varieties even more. In the green series, the Pied birds will have a yellow chest (as here) matching the ground colour of the head, mask, shoulders and wings. The expected green colour will be confined to the lower half of the body.

In the blue series, the chest will match the white of the head, mask, shoulders and wings. The lower body will be blue.

CANARIES

The canary is native to the Canary Islands, the Azores and Madeira. In the wild it is a flock-bird of the forests of these Atlantic islands. Unlike the budgerigar, the canary cannot tolerate drought and even in captivity it needs to drink and to bathe far more than the Australian birds.

In the late 15th century, the Spanish conquered the Canary Islands. Then began the trade in canaries, which were in demand throughout Europe for their song. The Spanish sold the male birds—the songsters—but never females. In this way, they kept the trade to themselves. No other Europeans could breed canaries until 1622. In that year, a ship with a cargo of canaries sank in the Mediterranean. Somehow the birds did not drown, but either escaped or were released by the crew. The canaries settled safely on the island of Elba and thrived. From this time other Europeans could breed canaries that had been caught there.

BORDER CANARY

Of the British-bred canaries, the Yorkshire, Norwich and the Border are most common. The Border, which was raised in the counties along the English–Scottish border, is a small, shapely canary, 14 cm long. A very good body outline is illustrated here. Colour, too, is thought important in this breed. Apart from yellow, white, buff, cinnamon and green, blue and fawn birds are also seen.

ROLLER CANARY

The Roller was bred in Germany, and is kept for its distinctive, soft song. The 'rolls' of the songs (bell-roll, water-roll, bass-roll, etc) are far more important than colouring or line. Buff or variegated plumage, as here, is quite common. Prize birds have been carefully trained by other Rollers called 'school-masters', but untrained Rollers are popular as very good, hardy pet birds.

GLOUCESTER CORONA

Another British breed is the Gloucester. These are slim but rounded birds, similar to the Border, but smaller. Yellow is usually mated to buff. The Corona (or Crest) is illustrated. The crest must be well-centred, blending with the neck feathers at the back, and not covering the eyes. The Gloucester Consort (or plainhead) lacks the crest, but is always mated to the Corona for best results.

Reptiles

Reptiles include the snakes, lizards, crocodiles, turtles, tortoises and terrapins. All are scaly skinned, backboned animals. They are cold blooded (i.e. relying on their surroundings for warmth) and they reproduce by laying eggs. Many people are fascinated by them, and good spotters will often find reptiles kept as pets. The trouble is that they cannot be recommended as pets. Those shown in this book are not meant to tempt anyone into trying to own one themselves.

Mediterranean Tortoises
The reptiles with most appeal as pets have been the Mediterranean tortoises. They have been imported in their millions throughout the century. The result has been that natural populations of the animal have died out, or are in danger of dying out. Fortunately, governments have listened to the pleas of conservationists and these tortoises may no longer be imported into any country that is a member state of the European Economic Community. This is good news, and no one should be disappointed that it is no longer possible to buy a Mediterranean tortoise in a pet shop.

Since the ban on the importation of Mediterranean tortoises, some traders have started to import other tortoises. The Horsfield's tortoise and the Carolina Box tortoise are two examples. They, too, are not suitable pets in cool climates. The ban will probably have to be extended to cover all tortoises, just to preserve the populations in the wild.

Terrapins
There is concern, too, over the importation of terrapins, although it is not illegal at present. The European pond terrapin (sometimes called a tortoise) is the most likely to survive as it still lives in the wild as far north as

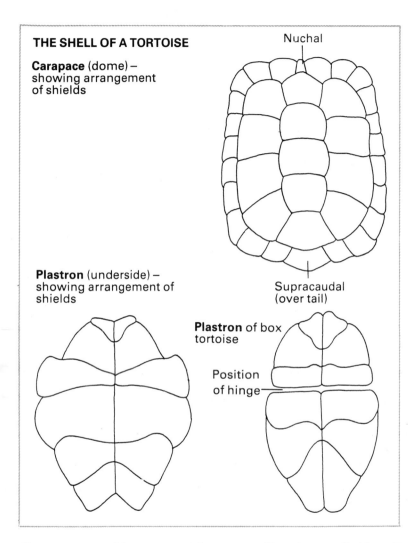

THE SHELL OF A TORTOISE

Carapace (dome) – showing arrangement of shields

Nuchal

Supracaudal (over tail)

Plastron (underside) – showing arrangement of shields

Plastron of box tortoise

Position of hinge

Germany, and long ago, when our climate was better, it lived wild in Britain. The Red-eared terrapin is a tropical species from the Gulf States of the USA. It is bred by the million in American 'terrapin farms' for export. Unfortunately, its chances of survival for any length of time are poor. It can only survive in a heated vivarium (a special heated tank) in this country.

TORTOISES

Tortoises are mainly herbivorous, although they probably eat small snails in the wild. In captivity their diet mainly consists of greenstuff. Many tortoises will also eat fruit and blossom.

To survive hibernation (a sleeping period lasting most of the winter months) a tortoise must feed well during the previous summer. If the weather is cool, it is sometimes possible to encourage it to eat by keeping it in a warm greenhouse or conservatory.

A box of hay or autumn leaves should be provided for hibernation. This can be insulated from frost by standing it in a bigger box with some packing material between the two. Keep it in a cool, dry place away from rats.

Check a hibernating tortoise during the early months of the year, and bring it out of hibernation as soon as it starts to move around. But keep it indoors until the weather warms up.

MEDITERRANEAN TORTOISES

The Greek, or spur-thighed tortoise (top). The shell may measure 30 cm in length, and the colour is usually pale brown with darker markings.

Hermann's tortoise (bottom) is also called the spur-tailed tortoise, with a claw-like spur at the tip of the tail. In size it is similar to the Greek. Some are dramatically coloured, as here.

HORSFIELD'S (Russian)

Horsfield's tortoise is native to the steppes of Asia, east of the Caspian Sea. It is small and rather circular in outline, and usually has a low-domed shell with a distinct green tinge. There

are four toes on each foot. Surprisingly, it is a very active climber and burrower. Indeed it will burrow every night if given the chance and not just for periods of hibernation. Because of this, it is difficult to contain except in a well-fenced, paved area. It is particularly fond of plants of the pea family, e.g. clover, and likes to bathe and drink from a shallow, sunken container of water that will not tip over.

CAROLINA BOX (American)

The Carolina Box is sometimes called a tortoise and at other times a terrapin. In fact, it is half-way between evolving into a tortoise from being a terrapin. As a result, it still has webbed feet. It has a high-domed shell, brightly marked with yellow. Males can be identified by their red eyes. Its hinged shell allows it to 'box' itself inside, with all the soft parts of the body protected when in danger, or when hibernating. The tortoise must have a pool to bathe in, but it is best kept in a good vivarium.

TERRAPINS

Unlike tortoises, terrapins are mainly carnivorous, although they will eat some greenstuff such as lettuce and water plants. Indeed they enjoy meat, fish (preferably whole fish), liver, other offal, mealworms and pond life such as water fleas (*Daphnia*) and *Tubifex* worms. If need be, crush the fish bones for small terrapins to provide a source of much-needed calcium. Meat and fish may have to be fed minced, or scraped, and lettuce may have to be shredded.

All terrapins need a pond with shallow sides so that they can easily climb on to a shore area or an island for basking. The European pond terrapin is difficult to confine, being extremely active and agile. It is wise to surround the pond and shore area with a wire enclosure.

The Red-eared terrapin can only be kept successfully in a vivarium, a special tank, heated to a minimum of 21°C.

RED-EARED TERRAPINS

This is a tropical terrapin which comes from America, and can only survive in Europe when kept in a heated vivarium throughout most of the year. Young specimens are bright green striped with yellow. The identification feature is a red spot behind the eye. The plastron (the shell covering its breast) is dramatically marked. Older specimens lose their colour, but survival rates are poor in Europe, and the older ones are not so often seen.

EUROPEAN POND TERRAPIN

This terrapin is native to Europe, and once even lived wild in Britain. It has a typical terrapin outline of low dome, webbed toes and long tail, and is a brownish-black colour. Some specimens are faintly green. The plastron is hinged and can be raised to encase the soft body in a safe 'box' when in danger or hibernating. The animal must have easy access to a pond.

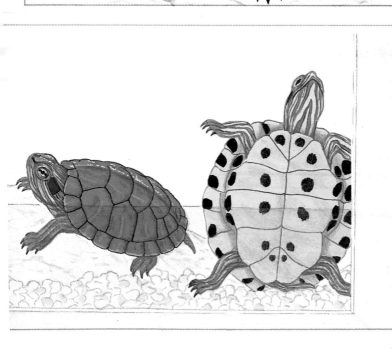

Fish

Hardy coldwater fish should be kept in a well-planted and carefully kept pond. The fish are then free to swim, to shelter from the light, to rest and to feed on natural foods such as water weeds and microscopic pond life.

In hot weather, fish are sometimes seen gasping at the surface of a small garden pond. This is a sign of oxygen starvation, and the remedy is to play a hosepipe or a sprinkler gently on the water.

In cold weather, fish may be trapped under a surface layer of ice. Breaking the ice would set up shock-waves that can kill fish. Sometimes it is possible to float pieces of wood or balls on the surface at night, and break them out in the morning. This opens up air holes for the fish, unless the day is very cold, in which case the holes will soon freeze over again. Usually, hardy fish will lie at the bottom of a frozen pond, too sluggish to swim or to feed. They will normally be safe if protected by 40–50 cm depth of water.

Autumn is the time to thin out fast-growing plants, which may overcrowd the pond. It is also the time to stretch a net across the surface to collect falling leaves before they clog up the pond. This is important, because the pond debris would decay under the ice.

Those varieties hardy enough to spend all year in a suitable pond include the Common goldfish, the Comet and the London Shubunkin. Less hardy fish must be kept in an aquarium, at least during the worst winter months. These include the Bristol Shubunkin, the Fantail and the Veiltail. The Black-eyed Moor must be kept in an aquarium permanently. It cannot see to feed properly in a pond, and its bulging eyes are in danger of being damaged.

A really large tank with a big surface area is essential if fish are to be kept in an aquarium. Under no circumstances should a small tank or a round glass bowl

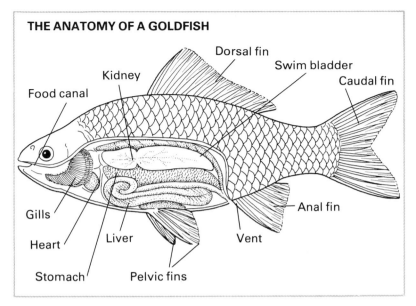

THE ANATOMY OF A GOLDFISH

Dorsal fin
Swim bladder
Kidney
Caudal fin
Food canal
Gills
Anal fin
Heart
Liver
Vent
Stomach
Pelvic fins

be used. A ventilated lid will keep dust off the water surface, and a layer of gravel on the bottom will allow pond weeds to take root. In turn these will provide welcome shade. Additionally in summer bright sunlight can be filtered out by screening the tank with a paper frieze. When feeding, only provide as much food as the fish use in a few minutes as unused food will just decay and make the need for cleaning more frequent.

Care of Goldfish
Plunging goldfish from water of one temperature into water of another can kill them; so it is important to remember this when changing the water of an aquarium. Freshly-drawn tap water should therefore be left to stand in buckets to warm up to room temperature before it is used. Try to change the water as little as possible, but always if it is looking cloudy, which indicates it is low in oxygen.

Fish should never be handled directly as this will damage the protective scale covering and a white fungus will often grow on the damaged tissue.

GOLDFISH

The Common goldfish is a member of the carp family. Originally it was a dull, greenish coloured fish, 'farmed' by the Chinese for food because it survived in small ponds where other fish would have died. Soon, in captivity, beautiful mutations appeared, and so its early use was forgotten and for centuries it was kept as an ornamental fish. It was first seen in Europe in the late 17th century and in Britain in the early 18th century.

About one hundred forms of fancy goldfish derive from the Common goldfish. They vary in body shape, size and colour, and in their fins. Most have lost some of the hardiness of the Common goldfish which can live for 25 years and reach a length of 40 cm (16 in). Fancy goldfish may live about 14 years.

Goldfish are social creatures, and two or three are better kept together than singly. But do not keep too many together as this will lead to overcrowding.

COMMON GOLDFISH

The colour varies from the intense red-gold of some fish, to the light golden colour of others. Young Common goldfish are born a dull, greenish-black, similar to the carp from which they are descended. Patches of black often persist for some years. Record the largest specimen you see, estimating its length without the tail fin. *Do not handle the fish.*

SHUBUNKINS

The Shubunkins are spectacular blue fish, with mottled marks of violet, red, yellow, brown and black. Two varieties have been bred. The hardier of the two, with the same outline as the Common goldfish, is the London. The other is the Bristol Shubunkin, with the forked, elongated tail fin of the Comet goldfish.

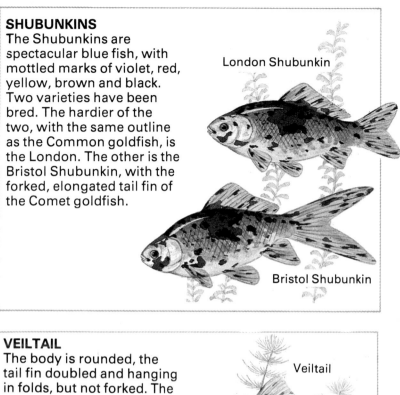

London Shubunkin

Bristol Shubunkin

VEILTAIL

The body is rounded, the tail fin doubled and hanging in folds, but not forked. The anal fins are paired.

BLACK-EYED MOOR

The body outline is exactly like the Veiltail. It is jet black in colour with bulging eyes.

FANTAIL

This has an egg-shaped body, with a deeply forked, double tail fin. Again the anal fins are paired.

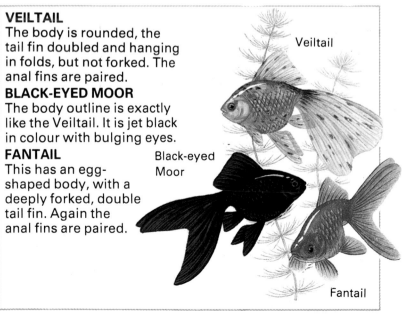

Veiltail

Black-eyed Moor

Fantail

Glossary

Amphibian animal living part of its life in water, part on land

Bi-coloured two-coloured

Carnivore animal feeding on flesh of other animals

Castration surgical removal of testicles (male reproductive parts)

Fancy animals animals bred to show certain desired characteristics for the show-bench

Hardy able to endure difficult conditions, e.g. low temperatures

Herbivore animal feeding on plants

Mammal animals which produce milk and can suckle their young

Nocturnal active at night

Offal edible parts of a carcass other than the flesh: liver, kidneys, heart, lungs, etc.

Pigment natural colouring matter

Predator animal which preys on another

Reptile cold-blooded animal with back bone and (usually) scaly skin

Rodent gnawing animal with growing incisors and no canine teeth

Spay surgical removal of uterus and/or ovaries (female reproductive parts)

Further Information

Index